DESTINATION SPACE

VISITING PLUTO:
The New Horizons Mission

Francis Spencer

A Crabtree Seedlings Book

Crabtree Publishing
crabtreebooks.com

Table of Contents

Our Solar System Loses a Planet.....5

Pluto.................................12

New Horizons, New Information.......18

Glossary...............................23

Index..................................23

Sun

Mercury

Venus

Earth

Mars

Our Solar System Loses a Planet

In our **solar system**, eight planets **orbit** a star we call the Sun.

Uranus

Neptune

Saturn

Jupiter

Earth is the third planet from the Sun in our solar system.

For many years, scientists had counted Pluto as a ninth planet in our solar system.

Sun

Pluto was discovered in 1930 by Clyde Tombaugh, an American astronomer.

Pluto

That changed in 2006. Scientists thought Pluto was too different from the other planets. They also learned it was more similar to other space objects. They renamed Pluto a dwarf planet.

One of the things that makes Pluto different from other planets is its size. Scientists consider it too small to be a true planet.

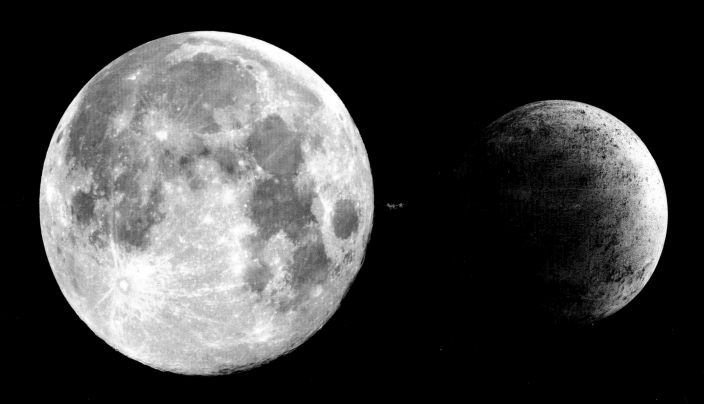

Pluto is slightly smaller than Earth's Moon.

Dwarf Planet Facts

- Dwarf planets are smaller than true planets.

- Dwarf planets orbit the Sun, but they share their orbits with other space objects. True planets do not share their orbits.

- Dwarf planets are round.

Haumea

Makemake

Ceres

Eris

Pluto

So far, five dwarf planets have been discovered and named by scientists.

Pluto

Pluto is over 3.6 billion miles (5.8 billion kilometers) away from the Sun, in a **region** called the Kuiper Belt.

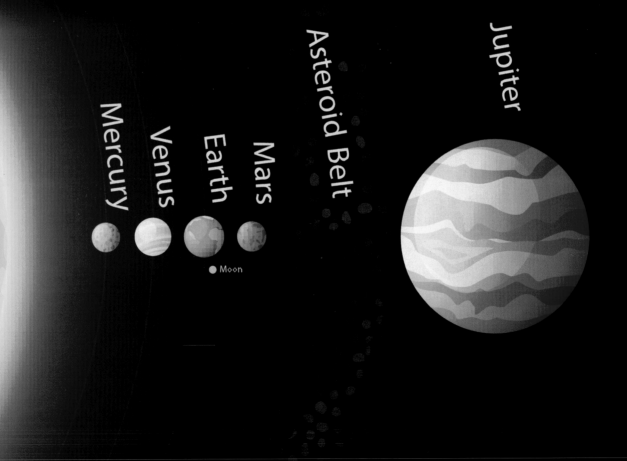

Mercury

Venus

Earth

Moon

Mars

Asteroid Belt

Jupiter

The Kuiper Belt is made up of comets, asteroids, and other space objects made mostly of ice.

Saturn

Uranus

Neptune

Kuiper Belt

Because it is so far away, it takes Pluto 248 years to orbit the Sun.

Sun

Pluto

248 Years

One day on Pluto is about six and a half days on Earth.

Scientists believe Pluto is made of mostly ice, with a small rocky **core**.

Temperatures on Pluto can plunge to -400 degrees Fahrenheit (-240 degrees Celsius).

Pluto's Moons

- Pluto has five known **moons**: Charon, Styx, Nix, Kerberos, and Hydra. (Kerberos and Styx were discovered by the Hubble Space Telescope in 2011 and 2012.)

- Charon is the largest of Pluto's moons.

- Charon is the closest moon to Pluto.

Pluto · Charon

New Horizons, New Information

In 2006, NASA launched *New Horizons*. It is a spacecraft able to take photos and gather information about Pluto and its moons.

The *New Horizons* spacecraft is about the size of a piano.

New Horizons

New Horizons has seven science tools on board. Some tools take photos; measure temperature and magnetic fields; map planet and moon surfaces; and study **atmospheres**. Other tools search for undiscovered moons and **subterranean** oceans.

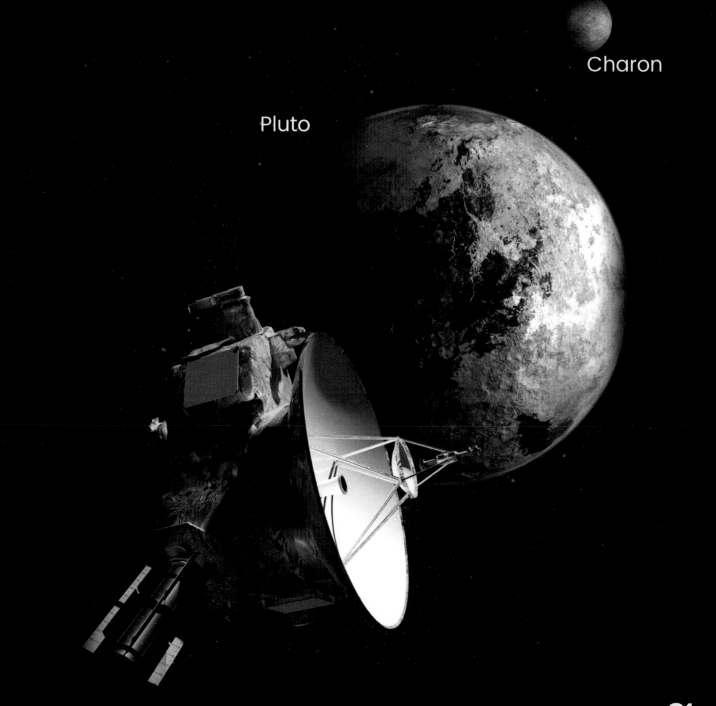

Charon

Pluto

21

Things we have learned from *New Horizons* include:

Pluto is 1,473 miles (2,370 kilometers) in diameter. It could fit across Earth's diameter at least five times.

We now know for sure Pluto is the largest of the known dwarf planets.

Pluto has mountains as high as 11,000 feet (3,353 meters).

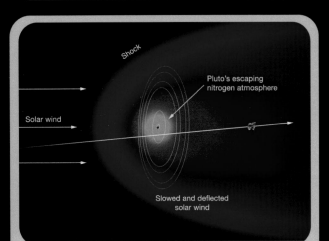

Pluto has a tail like a comet. This is caused by nitrogen leaking from its atmosphere into the solar wind.

Pluto's surface is much smoother, and therefore younger, than scientists had thought. Scientists believe Pluto's surface is still changing.

New Horizons should have enough power to last until 2026.

Glossary

atmosphere (AT-muhss-fihr): A layer of gases around a planet.

core (KOR): The center, or innermost layer.

moons (MOONZ): Natural satellites that orbit a planet.

orbit (OR-bit): To travel in an invisible path around a larger object such as a planet or star.

region (REE-juhn): An area.

solar system (SOH-luhr SIHS-tuhm): A star and all the planets and space objects that travel around it.

subterranean (suhb-tuh-RAYN-ee-uhn): Existing under the surface.

Index

astronomer 7

dwarf planet(s) 8, 10, 11, 22

Earth 4, 5, 9, 15, 20, 22

Kuiper Belt 12, 13

moon(s) 9, 17, 18, 20

NASA 18

New Horizons 18, 19, 20, 22

Sun 4, 5, 6, 10, 12, 14

solar system 5, 6

School-to-Home Support for Caregivers and Teachers

This book helps children grow by letting them practice reading. Here are a few guiding questions to help the reader build his or her comprehension skills. Possible answers appear here in red.

Before Reading

- **What do I think this book is about?** I think this book is about the planet Pluto. I think this book is about how far Pluto is from Earth.

- **What do I want to learn about this topic?** I want to learn why Pluto is now called a dwarf planet. I want to learn how people study Pluto.

During Reading

- **I wonder why...** I wonder why it is so cold on Pluto. I wonder why Pluto has tall mountains on its surface.

- **What have I learned so far?** I have learned that Pluto has five known moons. I have learned that scientists believe Pluto is made of mostly ice with a small rocky core.

After Reading

- **What details did I learn about this topic?** I have learned that Pluto has a tail like a comet. I have learned that it took the spacecraft *New Horizons* almost 10 years to reach Pluto.

- **Read the book again and look for the glossary words.** I see the word *orbit* on page 5, and the word *atmosphere* on page 20. The other glossary words are found on page 23.

Crabtree Publishing

crabtreebooks.com   800-387-7650

Copyright © 2022 Crabtree Publishing

We acknowledge the financial support of the Government of Canada through the Canada Book Fund for our publishing activities.

Hardcover   978-1-0396-4474-8
Paperback   978-1-0396-4665-0

Published in Canada
Crabtree Publishing
616 Welland Avenue
St. Catharines, Ontario
L2M 5V6

Published in the United States
Crabtree Publishing
347 Fifth Avenue
Suite 1402-145
New York, NY 10016

Written by: Francis Spencer
Print book version produced jointly with Blue Door Education in 2023

Photo Credits: Cover, title page and page 21 courtesy of Johns Hopkins University Applied Physics Laboratory/Southwest Research Institute (JHUAPL/SwRI); pages 4, 5, 6, 7, © Orla/Shutterstock.com; page 9 moon © dzika_mrowka/Shutterstock.com, Pluto page 16 © Vadim Sadovski/Shutterstock.comi; art page 10 and 17 © kasha_malasha/Shutterstock.com; page 11 courtesy of NASA; page 12, 13 © shooarts/Shutterstock.com; page 14 © ideyweb/Shutterstock.com; page 18 © Popova Valeriya/Shutterstock.com, page 19, 21, 22 © NASA/Johns Hopkins University Applied Physics Laboratory/Southwest Research Institute;

Library and Archives Canada
Cataloguing in Publication
Available at the Library and Archives Canada

Library of Congress
Cataloging-in-Publication Data
Available at the Library of Congress

Printed in Canada/102023/CPC20231018